Saint Joseph
GUIDE
FOR
Christian Prayer
(The Liturgy of the Hours)

For use with Edition No. 406

2024

No. 406/G

CATHOLIC BOOK PUBLISHING CORP.
New Jersey
catholicbookpublishing.com

The purpose of this handy GUIDE is to facilitate use of CHRISTIAN PRAYER, the one-volume **Liturgy of the Hours**, by providing clear, accurate references for each day of the year—always in accord with the principles on which this particular Breviary was compiled. These principles are enunciated on pages 34-37 of the volume and the use of this GUIDE is dependent upon a thorough understanding of these directives. Whenever a Saint is celebrated as a Memorial, the numbers in parentheses refer to the page in the Common that is to be used; the numbers without parentheses refer to the page in the Psalter that is to be used. (See p. 37 under Memorials.)

The designation **(New)** indicates that the Saint in question is found in the revised **SUPPLEMENT of the Liturgy of the Hours** (No. 405/04) published in 1992. **(No SUPPLEMENT** has been approved for publication since that time.). The designation *(New)* in lightface italics indicates that the Saint in question must be taken from the pertinent Common.

For those who will use the Edition with Music and the Office of Readings, the pertinent information is supplied on a separate line within brackets at the end of each entry.

LIST OF ABBREVIATIONS

Ab — Abbot
Ant — Antiphon
Ap — Apostle
B, Bb — Bishop(s)
Bl. — Blessed
BVM — Blessed Virgin Mary
Comp(s) — Companion(s)
D, Dd — Doctor(s)
De — Deacon
Ded — Dedication of Church
DP — Daytime Prayer
EP — Evening Prayer
F — Feast
f — following page(s)
M, Mm — Martyr(s)

Mem — Memorial (Obligatory)
Miss — Missionaries
MP — Morning Prayer
NP — Night Prayer
OOR — Office of Readings
P, Pp — Priest(s)
Po — Pope
Pr — Prayer
Rd — Reading(s)
Rel — Religious
Sol — Solemnity
St., Sts. — Saint(s)
TD — Te Deum
V — Virgin

(406/G)

JANUARY

EP 173 (1368); NP 1034 or 1037

1. **Mon. MARY, MOTHER OF GOD (Sol) 175**
   MP 175 (707); DP 1027; EP 178; NP 1037
   [OOR 1788, Rd 1882f & 1951f; TD Pr 175]

2. Tue. Sts. Basil the Great and Gregory Nazianzen, Bb & Dd (Mem) 1060
   MP (1426 or 1434) (Ant) 728; DP 1003
   EP (1430 or 1436) (Ant) 734; NP 1044
   [OOR 1791, Rd 1882f & 2046f; Pr 1060]

3. Wed. Wednesday before Epiphany or The Most Holy Name of Jesus *(New)*
   No official texts exist yet in English.
   MP (195) 738; DP 1008; EP (196) 743; NP 1046
   [OOR 1794, Rd 1882f & 1955f; Pr 196]

4. Thu. St. Elizabeth Ann Seton (Mem) 1061
   MP (1470) 748; DP 1012; EP (1471) 754; NP 1049
   [OOR 1797, Rd 1882f & 2049f; Pr 1061]

5. Fri. St. John Neumann, B (Mem) 1062
   MP (1426) 759; DP 1017; EP (1430) 765; NP 1052
   [OOR 1800, Rd 1882f & 2046f; Pr 1062]

6. Sat. Saturday before Epiphany or St. André Bessette, Rel **(New)** (5)
   MP (205) (1470) 770, Pr proper (6) or 1471; DP 1022
   EP 207; NP 1034
   [OOR 1802, Rd 1882f & 1955f or 2049f; Pr (6) or 1471 or 206]

7. **Sun. EPIPHANY (Sol) 211**
   MP 211 (707); DP 1027; EP 214; NP 1037
   [OOR 1806, Rd 1882f & 1965f; TD Pr 211]

8. Mon. BAPTISM OF THE LORD (F) 239
   MP 239 (707); DP 998; EP 242 (214); NP 1041
   [OOR 1809, Rd 1882f & 1966f; TD Pr 241]

9. Tue. Tuesday of the 1st Week in Ordinary Time
   MP 728; DP 1003; EP 734; NP 1044
   [OOR 1791, Rd 1924f & 2011f; Pr 245]

10. Wed. Wednesday of the 1st Week in Ordinary Time
    MP 738; DP 1008; EP 743; NP 1046
    [OOR 1794, Rd 1924f & 2011f; Pr 245]

11. Thu. Thursday of the 1st Week in Ordinary Time
MP 748; DP 1012; EP 754; NP 1049
[OOR 1797, Rd 1924f & 2011f; Pr 245]

12. Fri. Friday of the 1st Week in Ordinary Time
MP 759; DP 1017; EP 765; NP 1052
[OOR 1800, Rd 1924f & 2011f; Pr 245]

13. Sat. Weekday or St. Hilary, B & D (1063) or BVM on Saturday (1383)
MP (1426 or 1434) (1383) 770; DP 1022; EP (246) 775; NP 1034
[OOR 1802, Rd 1924f & 2011f or 2046f or 2051f; Pr 1064 or 1386 or 245]

14. **Sun. SECOND SUNDAY IN ORDINARY TIME 246**
MP 780; DP 994; EP 786; NP 1037
[OOR 1806, Rd 1924f & 2011f; TD Pr 246]

15. Mon. Monday of the 2nd Week in Ordinary Time
MP 792; DP 998; EP 798; NP 1041
[OOR 1809, Rd 1924f & 2011f; Pr 246]

16. Tue. Tuesday of the 2nd Week in Ordinary Time
MP 802; DP 1003; EP 807; NP 1044
[OOR 1812, Rd 1924f & 2011f; Pr 246]

17. Wed. St. Anthony, Ab (Mem) 1064
MP (1470) 812; DP 1008; EP (1471) 818; NP 1046
[OOR 1816, Rd 1924f & 2049f; Pr 1064]

18. Thu. Thursday of the 2nd Week in Ordinary Time
MP 824; DP 1012; EP 830; NP 1049
[OOR 1819, Rd 1924f & 2011f; Pr 246]

19. Fri. Friday of the 2nd Week in Ordinary Time
MP 835; DP 1017; EP 840; NP 1052
[OOR 1821, Rd 1924f & 2011f; Pr 246]

20. Sat. Weekday or St. Fabian, Po & M or St. Sebastian, M (1065) or BVM
on Saturday (1383)
MP (1414 or 1426) 845; DP 1022; EP 851 (247); NP 1034
[OOR 1824, Rd 1924f & 2011f or 2045f or 1951f; Pr 1065 or 1386 or 246]

21. **Sun. THIRD SUNDAY IN ORDINARY TIME 247**
MP 856; DP 994; EP 861; NP 1037
[OOR 1827, Rd 1924f & 2011f; TD Pr 247]

22. Mon. Day of Prayer for the Legal Protection of Unborn Children
MP 867; DP 998; EP 872; NP 1041
[OOR 1829, Rd 1924f & 2011f; Pr 247]

23.   Tue. Weekday or St. Vincent, De & M (1068) **[transferred from 1/22]**
       or St. Marianne Cope, V *(New)* (1441 or 1472)
    MP (1414) (1441 or 1472) 877; DP 1003
    EP (1417) (1444 or 1472) 882; NP 1044
    [OOR 1831, Rd 1924f & 2011f or 2045f or 2048f; Pr 1068 or 1472 or 247]

24.   Wed. St. Francis de Sales, B & D (Mem) 1068
    MP (1426 or 1434) 886; DP 1008; EP (1430 or 1436) 892; NP 1046
    [OOR 1835, Rd 1924f & 2046f; Pr 1069]

25.   Thu. CONVERSION OF ST. PAUL, AP (F) 1069
    MP 1069 (707); DP 1012; EP 1071 (1394); NP 1049
    [OOR 1838, Rd 1924f & 2043f; TD Pr 1071]

26.   Fri. Sts. Timothy and Titus, Bb (Mem) 1073
    MP (1426) (Ant) 906; DP 1017; EP (1430) (Ant) 911; NP 1052
    [OOR 1842, Rd 1924f & 2046f; Pr 1073]

27.   Sat. Weekday or St. Angela Merici, V (1074) or BVM on Sat. (1383)
    MP (1441 or 1473) (1383) 916; DP 1022; EP 921 (248); NP 1034
    [OOR 1845, Rd 1924f & 2011f or 2048f or 1951f; Pr 1074 or 247]

28.   **Sun. FOURTH SUNDAY IN ORDINARY TIME 248**
    MP 925; DP 994; EP 931; NP 1037
    [OOR 1850, Rd 1924f & 2011f; TD Pr 248]

29.   Mon. Monday of the 4th Week in Ordinary Time
    MP 937; DP 998; EP 942; NP 1041
    [OOR 1853, Rd 1924f & 2011f; Pr 248]

30.   Tue. Tuesday of the 4th Week in Ordinary Time
    MP 947; DP 1003; EP 953; NP 1044
    [OOR 1856, Rd 1924f & 2011f; Pr 248]

31.   Wed. St. John Bosco, P (Mem) 1076
    MP (1426 or 1473) 958; DP 1008; EP (1430 or 1473) 963; NP 1046
    [OOR 1859, Rd 1924f & 2046f; Pr 1076]

FEBRUARY

1.   Thu. Thursday of the 4th Week in Ordinary Time
    MP 968; DP 1012; EP 973; NP 1049
    [OOR 1861, Rd 1924f & 2011f; Pr 248]

2.   Fri. PRESENTATION OF THE LORD (F) 1081
MP 1081 (707); DP 1017; EP 1082; NP 1052
[OOR 1864, Rd 1924f & 2011f; TD Pr 1082]

3.   Sat. Weekday or St. Blase, B & M (1086) or St. Ansgar, B (1087) or
BVM on Saturday (1383)
MP (1414 or 1426) (1426) (1383) 988; DP 1022
EP 701 (249); NP 1034
[OOR 1867, Rd 1924f & 2011f or 2045f or 2046f, or 1951f; Pr 1086 or
1087 or 1386 or 248]

4.   **Sun. FIFTH SUNDAY IN ORDINARY TIME 249**
MP 706; DP 994; EP 712; NP 1037
[OOR 1785, Rd 1924f & 2011f; TD Pr 249]

5.   Mon. St. Agatha, V & M (Mem) 1087
MP (1414 or 1441) (Ant) 718; DP 998
EP (1417 or 1444) (Ant) 723; NP 1041
[OOR 1788, Rd 1924f & 2045f or 2048f; Pr 1088]

6.   Tue. St. Paul Miki and Comps, Mm (Mem) 1088
MP (1402) (Ant) 728; DP 1003; EP (1405) (Ant) 734; NP 1044
[OOR 1791, Rd 1924f & 2045f; Pr 1089]

7.   Wed. Wednesday of the 5th Week in Ordinary Time
MP 738; DP 1008; EP 743; NP 1046
[OOR 1794, Rd 1924f & 2011f; Pr 249]

8.   Thu. Weekday or St. Jerome Emiliani (1089) or St. Josephine Bakhita, V
(New) (1441)
MP (1473) (1441) (Ant) 748; DP 1012
EP (1473) (1444) (Ant) 754; NP 1049
[OOR 1797, Rd 1924f & 2011f or 2049f or 2048f; Pr 1090 or 1443 or 249]

9.   Fri. Friday of the 5th Week in Ordinary Time
MP 759; DP 1017; EP 765; NP 1052
[OOR 1800, Rd 1924f & 2011f; Pr 249]

10.   Sat. St. Scholastica, V (Mem) 1090
MP (1441) (Ant) 770; DP 1022; EP 775 (250); NP 1034
[OOR 1802, Rd 1924f & 2048f; Pr 1091]

11.   **Sun. SIXTH SUNDAY IN ORDINARY TIME 250**
MP 780; DP 994; EP 786; NP 1037
[OOR 1806, Rd 1924f & 2011f; TD Pr 250]

12.   Mon. Monday of the 6th Week in Ordinary Time
      MP 792; DP 998; EP 798; NP 1041
      [OOR 1809, Rd 1924f & 2011f; Pr 250]

13.   Tue. Tuesday of the 6th Week in Ordinary Time
      MP 802; DP 1003; EP 807; NP 1044
      [OOR 1812, Rd 1924f & 2011f; Pr 250]

14.   Wed. ASH WEDNESDAY 255
      MP (255) 906 or 958; DP 1008; EP (256) 963; NP 1046
      [OOR 1859, Rd 1890f & 1968f; Pr 256]

15.   Thu. Thursday after Ash Wednesday
      MP (258) 968; DP 1012; EP (259) 973; NP 1049
      [OOR 1861, Rd 1890f & 1968f; Pr 259]

16.   Fri. Friday after Ash Wednesday
      MP (261) 978; DP 1017; EP (262) 984; NP 1052
      [OOR 1864, Rd 1890f & 1968f; Pr 262]

17.   Saturday after Ash Wednesday
      MP (264) 988 (Seven Founders of the Order of Servites 1093); DP 1022
      EP (266) 701; NP 1034
      [OOR 1867, Rd 1890f & 1968f; Pr 1093 or 265]

18.   **Sun. FIRST SUNDAY OF LENT 268**
      MP (268) 707; DP 994; EP (270) 712; NP 1037
      [OOR 1785, Rd 1890f & 1973f; Pr 269]

19.   Mon. Monday of the 1st Week of Lent
      MP (272) 718; DP 998; EP (273) 723; NP 1041
      [OOR 1788, Rd 1890f & 1968f; Pr 273]

20.   Tue. Tuesday of the 1st Week of Lent
      MP (275) 728; DP 1003; EP (276) 734; NP 1044
      [OOR 1791, Rd 1890f & 1968f; Pr 276]

21.   Wed. Wednesday of the 1st Week of Lent
      MP (278) 738 (St. Peter Damian, B & D 1094); DP 1008
      EP (280) 743 (St. Peter Damian, B & D 1095); NP 1046
      [OOR 1794, Rd 1890f & 1968f; Pr 1095 or 279]

22.   Thu. CHAIR OF ST. PETER, AP (F) 1095
      MP 1095 (707); DP 1012; EP 1097 (1394); NP 1049
      [OOR 1797, Rd 1890f & 2043f; TD Pr 1097]

23. Fri. Friday of the 1st Week of Lent
MP (285) 759 (St. Polycarp, B & M 1100); DP 1017
EP (286) 765 (St. Polycarp, B & M 1100); NP 1052
[OOR 1800, Rd 1890f & 1968f; Pr 1100 or 286]

24. Sat. Saturday of the 1st Week of Lent
MP (288) 770; DP 1022; EP (290) 775; NP 1034
[OOR 1802, Rd 1890f & 1968f; Pr 289]

25. **Sun. SECOND SUNDAY OF LENT 292**
MP (292) 781; DP 994; EP (294) 786; NP 1037
[OOR 1806, Rd 1890f & 1977f; Pr 293]

26. Mon. Monday of the 2nd Week of Lent
MP (296) 792; DP 998; EP (297) 798; NP 1041
[OOR 1809, Rd 1890f & 1968f; Pr 297]

27. Tue. Tuesday of the 2nd Week of Lent
MP (299) 802 (Ant of St. Gregory of Narek p. 39 of this Guide & Pr
1435 or 1471); DP 1003
EP (301) 807 (Ant of St. Gregory of Narek p. 39 of this Guide & Pr
1435 or 1471); NP 1044
[OOR 1812, Rd 1890f & 1968f; Pr 300 or 1435 or 1471]

28. Wed. Wednesday of the 2nd Week of Lent
MP (302) 812; DP 1008; EP (304) 818; NP 1046
[OOR 1816, Rd 1890f & 1968f; Pr 304]

29. Thu. Thursday of the 2nd Week of Lent
MP (306) 824; DP 1012; EP (307) 830; NP 1049
[OOR 1819, Rd 1890f & 1968f; Pr 307]

MARCH

1. Fri. Friday of the 2nd Week of Lent
MP (309) 835; DP 1017; EP (310) 840; NP 1052
[OOR 1821, Rd 1890f & 1968f; Pr 310]

2. Sat. Saturday of the 2nd Week of Lent
MP (312) 845; DP 1022; EP (314) 851; NP 1034
[OOR 1824, Rd 1890f & 1968f; Pr 313]

3. **Sun. THIRD SUNDAY OF LENT 316**
MP (316) 856; DP 994; EP (318) 861; NP 1037
[OOR 1827, Rd 1890f & 1968f; Pr 317]

4.   Mon. Monday of the 3rd Week of Lent
MP (320) 867 (St. Casimir 1101); DP 998
EP (322) 872 (St. Casimir 1101); NP 1041
[OOR 1829, Rd 1890f & 1968f; Pr 1101 or 321]

5.   Tue. Tuesday of the 3rd Week of Lent
MP (323) 877; DP 1003; EP (324) 882; NP 1044
[OOR 1831, Rd 1890f & 1968f; Pr 324]

6.   Wed. Wednesday of the 3rd Week of Lent
MP (326) 886; DP 1008; EP (328) 892; NP 1046
[OOR 1835, Rd 1890f & 1968f; Pr 327]

7.   Thu. Thursday of the 3rd Week of Lent
MP (329) 897 (Sts. Perpetua and Felicity, Mm 1102); DP 1012
EP (331) 901 (Sts. Perpetua and Felicity, Mm 1102); NP 1049
[OOR 1838, Rd 1890f & 1968f; Pr 1102 or 330]

8.   Fri. Friday of the 3rd Week of Lent
MP (332) 906 (St. John of God, Rel 1103); DP 1017
EP (334) 911 (St. John of God, Rel 1103); NP 1052
[OOR 1842, Rd 1890f & 1968f; Pr 1103 or 333]

9.   Sat. Saturday of the 3rd Week of Lent
MP (335) 916 (St. Frances of Rome, Rel 1104); DP 1022
EP (338) 921; NP 1034
[OOR 1845, Rd 1890f & 1968f; Pr 1104 or 337]

10.   **Sun. FOURTH SUNDAY OF LENT 340**
MP (340) 925; DP 994; EP (342) 931; NP 1037
[OOR 1850, Rd 1890f & 1968f; Pr 341]

11.   Mon. Monday of the 4th Week of Lent
MP (344) 937; DP 998; EP (346) 942; NP 1041
[OOR 1853, Rd 1890f & 1968f; Pr 346]

12.   Tue. Tuesday of the 4th Week of Lent
MP (347) 947; DP 1003; EP (349) 953; NP 1044
[OOR 1856, Rd 1890f & 1968f; Pr 349]

13.   Wed. Wednesday of the 4th Week of Lent
MP (351) 958; DP 1008; EP (352) 963; NP 1046
[OOR 1859, Rd 1890f & 1968f; Pr 352]

14. Thu. Thursday of the 4th Week of Lent
MP (354) 968; DP 1012; EP (355) 973; NP 1049
[OOR 1861, Rd 1890f & 1968f; Pr 355]

15. Fri. Friday of the 4th Week of Lent
MP (357) 978; DP 1017; EP (358) 984; NP 1052
[OOR 1864, Rd 1890f & 1968f; Pr 358]

16. Sat. Saturday of the 4th Week of Lent
MP (360) 988; DP 1022; EP (362) 701; NP 1034
[OOR 1867, Rd 1890f & 1968f; Pr 361]

17. **Sun. FIFTH SUNDAY OF LENT 364**
MP (364) 707; DP 994; EP (366) 712; NP 1037
[OOR 1785, Rd 1890f & 1968f; Pr 365]

18. Mon. Monday of the 5th Week of Lent
MP (368) 718 (St. Cyril of Jerusalem, B & D 1106); DP 998
EP 1107 (1448); NP 1034
[OOR 1788, Rd 1890f & 1968f; Pr 1106 or 369]

19. Tue. ST. JOSEPH, HUSBAND OF MARY (Sol) 1109
MP 1109 (707); DP 1027; EP 1111; NP 1037
[OOR 1791, Rd 1890f & 2055f; TD Pr 1110]

20. Wed. Wednesday of the 5th Week of Lent
MP (374) 738; DP 1008; EP (376) 743; NP 1046
[OOR 1794, Rd 1890f & 1968f; Pr 375]

21. Thu. Thursday of the 5th Week of Lent
MP (377) 748; DP 1012; EP (379) 754; NP 1049
[OOR 1797, Rd 1890f & 1968f; Pr 378]

22. Fri. Friday of the 5th Week of Lent
MP (380) 759; DP 1017; EP (382) 765; NP 1052
[OOR 1800, Rd 1890f & 1968f; Pr 381]

23. Sat. Saturday of the 5th Week of Lent
MP (383) 770 (St. Turibius de Mogrovejo, B 1113); DP 1022
EP (386) 775; NP 1034
[OOR 1802, Rd 1890f & 1968f; Pr 1113 or 384]

24. **Sun. PASSION SUNDAY (PALM SUNDAY) 388**
MP (388) 780; DP 994; EP (390) 786; NP 1037
[OOR 1806, Rd 1890f & 1979f; Pr 390]

25. Mon. MONDAY OF HOLY WEEK
     MP (393) 792; DP 998; EP (395) 798; NP 1041
     [OOR 1809, Rd 1890f & 1981f; Pr 394]

26. Tue. TUESDAY OF HOLY WEEK
     MP (397) 802; DP 1003; EP (398) 807; NP 1044
     [OOR 1812, Rd 1890f & 1985f; Pr 398]

27. Wed. WEDNESDAY OF HOLY WEEK
     MP (400) 812; DP 1008; EP (402) 818; NP 1046
     [OOR 1816, Rd 1890f & 1981f or 1985f; Pr 402]

28. Thu. HOLY THURSDAY 404
     MP 824 (404); DP 1012; EP 830 (406); NP 1037
     [OOR 1819, Rd 1890f & 1982f; Pr 405]

29. Fri. GOOD FRIDAY 408
     MP 408; DP 1017; EP 413; NP 1037
     [OOR 1821, Rd 1890f & 1984f; Pr 413]

30. Sat. HOLY SATURDAY 417
     MP 417; DP 1022; EP 422; NP 1037
     [OOR 1824, Rd 1890f & 1987f; Pr 421]

31. **Sun. EASTER SUNDAY 427**
     MP 427 (707); DP 994; EP 429; NP 1037
     [OOR 1785, Rd 1910f & 1989f; TD Pr 428]

APRIL

1. Mon. MONDAY WITHIN THE OCTAVE OF EASTER
    MP 427 & 434; DP 998; EP 429 & 435; NP 1034 or 1037
    [OOR 1788, Rd 1910f & 1989f; TD Pr 435]

2. Tue. TUESDAY WITHIN THE OCTAVE OF EASTER
    MP 427 & 437; DP 1003; EP 429 & 438; NP 1034 or 1037
    [OOR 1791, Rd 1910f & 1989f; TD Pr 438]

3. Wed. WEDNESDAY WITHIN THE OCTAVE OF EASTER
    MP 427 & 440; DP 1008; EP 429 & 441; NP 1034 or 1037
    [OOR 1794, Rd 1910f & 1989f; TD Pr 441]

4. Thu. THURSDAY WITHIN THE OCTAVE OF EASTER
    MP 427 & 443; DP 1012; EP 429 & 444; NP 1034 or 1037
    [OOR 1797, Rd 1910f & 1989f; TD Pr 444]

5. Fri. FRIDAY WITHIN THE OCTAVE OF EASTER
MP 427 & 446; DP 1017; EP 429 & 447; NP 1034 or 1037
[OOR 1800, Rd 1910f & 1989f; TD Pr 447]

6. Sat. SATURDAY WITHIN THE OCTAVE OF EASTER
MP 427 & 449; DP 1022; EP 429 & 451; NP 1034 or 1037
[OOR 1802, Rd 1910f & 1989f; TD Pr 450]

7. **Sun. SECOND SUNDAY OF EASTER 453**
MP 427 & 453; DP 994; EP 429 & 455; NP 1037
[OOR 1806, Rd 1910f & 1995f; TD Pr 454]

8. Mon. ANNUNCIATION OF THE LORD (Sol) 1118 **(transferred from 3/25)**
MP 1118 (707); DP 1027; EP 1120; NP 1037
[OOR 1809, Rd 1910f & 1956f; TD Pr 1119]

9. Tue. Tuesday of the 2nd Week of Easter
MP (460) 802; DP 1003; EP (461) 807; NP 1044
[OOR 1812, Rd 1910f & 1989f; Pr 461]

10. Wed. Wednesday of the 2nd Week of Easter
MP (463) 812; DP 1008; EP (464) 818; NP 1046
[OOR 1816, Rd 1910f & 1989f; Pr 464]

11. Thu. St. Stanislaus, B & M (Mem) 1128
MP (1414 or 1426) (Ant) 824; DP 1012
EP (1417 or 1430) (Ant) 830; NP 1049
[OOR 1819, Rd 1910f & 2045f or 2046f; Pr 1128]

12. Fri. Friday of the 2nd Week of Easter
MP (468) 835; DP 1017; EP (470) 840; NP 1052
[OOR 1821, Rd 1910f & 1989f; Pr 470]

13. Sat. Easter Weekday or St. Martin I, Po & M (1129)
MP (1414 or 1426) (Ant) (471) 845; DP 1022
EP (474) 851; NP 1034
[OOR 1824, Rd 1910f & 1989f or 2045f or 2046f; Pr 1129 or 473]

14. **Sun. THIRD SUNDAY OF EASTER 476**
MP (476) 856; DP 994; EP (478) 861; NP 1037
[OOR 1827, Rd 1910f & 1989f; TD Pr 477]

15. Mon. Monday of the 3rd Week of Easter
MP (480) 867; DP 998; EP (481) 872; NP 1041
[OOR 1829, Rd 1910f & 1989f; Pr 481]

16.　Tue. Tuesday of the 3rd Week of Easter
　　MP (483) 877; DP 1003; EP (484) 882; NP 1044
　　[OOR 1831, Rd 1910f & 1989f; Pr 484]

17.　Wed. Wednesday of the 3rd Week of Easter
　　MP (486) 886; DP 1008; EP (487) 892; NP 1046
　　[OOR 1835, Rd 1910f & 1989f; Pr 487]

18.　Thu. Thursday of the 3rd Week of Easter
　　MP (489) 897; DP 1012; EP (490) 901; NP 1049
　　[OOR 1838, Rd 1910f & 1989f; Pr 490]

19.　Fri. Friday of the 3rd Week of Easter
　　MP (491) 906; DP 1017; EP (493) 911; NP 1052
　　[OOR 1842, Rd 1910f & 1989f; Pr 492]

20.　Sat. Saturday of the 3rd Week of Easter
　　MP (494) 916; DP 1022; EP (496) 921; NP 1034
　　[OOR 1845, Rd 1910f & 1989f; Pr 495]

21.　**Sun. FOURTH SUNDAY OF EASTER 498**
　　MP (498) 925; DP 994; EP (500) 931; NP 1037
　　[OOR 1850, Rd 1910f & 1989f; TD Pr 499]

22.　Mon. Monday of the 4th Week of Easter
　　MP (502) 937; DP 998; EP (503) 942; NP 1041
　　[OOR 1853, Rd 1910f & 1989f; Pr 503]

23.　Tue. Easter Weekday or St. George, M (1130) or St. Adalbert, B & M
　　　(New) (1426 or 1414)
　　MP (1414) (1426 or 1414) (505) 947; DP 1003
　　EP (1417) (1430 or 1417) (506) 953; NP 1044
　　[OOR 1856, Rd 1910f & 1989f or 2045f or 2046f; Pr 1131 or 1416 or 1428
　　　or 506]

24.　Wed. Easter Weekday or St. Fidelis of Sigmaringen, P & M (1131)
　　　MP (1414 or 1426) (508) 958; DP 1008
　　　EP (1417 or 1430) (509) 963; NP 1046
　　　[OOR 1859, Rd 1910f & 1989f or 2045f; Pr 1131 or 509]

25.　Thu. ST. MARK, EVANGELIST (F) 1132
　　　MP 1132 (707); DP 1012; EP 1134 (1394); NP 1049
　　　[OOR 1861, Rd 1910f & 2043f; TD Pr 1134]

26. Fri. Friday of the 4th Week of Easter
    MP (514) 978; DP 1017; EP (515) 984; NP 1052
    [OOR 1864, Rd 1910f & 1989f; Pr 515]

27. Sat. Saturday of the 4th Week of Easter
    MP (517) 988; DP 1022; EP (519) 701; NP 1034
    [OOR 1867, Rd 1910f & 1989f; Pr 518]

28. **Sun. FIFTH SUNDAY OF EASTER 521**
    MP (521) 707; DP 994; EP (523) 712; NP 1037
    [OOR 1785, Rd 1910f & 1989f; TD Pr 522]

29. Mon. St. Catherine of Siena, V & D (Mem) 1136
    MP (1441) (Ant) 718: DP 998; EP (1444) (Ant) 723; NP 1041
    [OOR 1788, Rd 1910f & 2048f; Pr 1137]

30. Tue. Easter Weekday or St. Pius V, Po (1137)
    MP (1426) (528) 728; DP 1003; EP (1430) (529) 734; NP 1044
    [OOR 1791, Rd 1910f & 1989f or 2046f; Pr 1138 or 529]

MAY

1. Wed. Easter Weekday or St. Joseph the Worker (1139)
   MP (1139) (531) 738; DP 1008; EP (1140) (532) 743; NP 1046
   [OOR 1794, Rd 1910f & 1989f or 2055f; Pr 1140 or 532]

2. Thu. St. Athanasius, B & D (Mem) 1142
   MP (1426 or 1435) 748; DP 1012
   EP (1430 or 1436) 754; NP 1049
   [OOR 1797, Rd 1910f & 2046f; Pr 1142]

3. Fri. STS. PHILIP AND JAMES, AP (F) 1143
   MP 1143 (707); DP 1017; EP 1145 (1394); NP 1052
   [OOR 1800, Rd 1910f & 2043f; TD Pr 1145]

4. Sat. Saturday of the 5th Week of Easter
   MP (539) 770; DP 1022; EP (541) 775; NP 1034
   [OOR 1802, Rd 1910f & 1989f; Pr 540]

5. **Sun. SIXTH SUNDAY OF EASTER 543**
   MP (543) 780; DP 994; EP (545) 786; NP 1037
   [OOR 1806, Rd 1910f & 1989f; TD Pr 544]

6. Mon. Monday of the 6th Week of Easter
   MP (547) 792; DP 998; EP (548) 798; NP 1041
   [OOR 1809, Rd 1910f & 1989f; Pr 548]

7. Tue. Tuesday of the 6th Week of Easter
    MP (549) 802; DP 1003; EP (551) 807; NP 1044
    [OOR 1812, Rd 1910f & 1989f; Pr 551]

8. Wed. Wednesday of the 6th Week of Easter
    MP (552) 812; DP 1008; EP 559; NP 1034
    [OOR 1816, Rd 1910f & 1989f; Pr 554]

9. **Thu. ASCENSION (Sol) 562**
    MP (563) 707; DP 1027; EP 565; NP 1037
    [OOR 1819, Rd 1910f & 2005f; TD Pr 562]

10. Fri. Easter Weekday or St. John of Avila, P & D *(New)* (1426 or 1435) or
    St. Damien de Veuster of Moloka'i, P *(New)* (1426)
    MP (1426 or 1435) (1426) (569) 835; DP 1017; EP (1430 or 1436)
    (1430) (571) 840; NP 1052
    [OOR 1821, Rd 1910f & 1989f or 2046f; Pr 1429 or 1435 or 571]

11. Sat. Saturday of the 6th Week of Easter
    MP (574) 845; DP 1022; EP (577) 851; NP 1034
    [OOR 1824, Rd 1910f & 1989f; Pr 576]

12. **Sun. SEVENTH SUNDAY OF EASTER 579**
    MP (579) 856; DP 994; EP (581) 861; NP 1037
    [OOR 1827, Rd 1910f & 1989f; TD Pr 580]

WHERE THE ASCENSION IS NOT TO BE OBSERVED AS A HOLYDAY OF OBLIGA-
TION, IT IS ASSIGNED TO THE SEVENTH SUNDAY OF EASTER. **The specified
rubrics below are to be followed until Monday of the 7th Week of Easter.**

8. Wed. Wednesday of the 6th Week of Easter
    MP (552) 812; DP 1008; EP (554) 818; NP 1046
    [OOR 1816, Rd 1910f & 1989f; Pr 554]

9. Thu. Thursday of the 6th Week of Easter
    MP (556) 824; DP 1012; EP (557) 830; NP 1049
    [OOR 1819, Rd 1910f & 1989f; Pr 557]

10. Fri. Easter Weekday or St. John of Avila, P & D *(New)* (1426 or 1435) or
    St. Damien de Veuster of Moloka'i, P *(New)* (1426)
    MP (1426 or 1435) (1426) (569) 835; DP 1017; EP (1430 or 1436)
    (1430) (571) 840; NP 1052
    [OOR 1821, Rd 1910f & 1989f or 2046f; Pr 1429 or 1435 or 571]

11. Sat. Saturday of the 6th Week of Easter
    MP (574) 845; DP 1022; EP 559; NP 1034
    [OOR 1824, Rd 1910f & 1989f; Pr 575]

12. **Sun. ASCENSION (Sol) 562**
    MP (563) 707; DP 1027; EP 565; NP 1037
    [OOR 1827, Rd 1910f & 2005f; TD Pr 562]

13. Mon. Easter Weekday or Our Lady of Fatima *(New)* Common of the Blessed Virgin Mary (1372)
    MP (583) (1372) 867; DP 998; EP (584) (1378) 872; NP 1041
    [OOR 1829, Rd 1910f & 1989f or 1951f; Pr 1376 or 584]

14. Tue. ST. MATTHIAS, AP (F) 1148
    MP 1392 (Ant) (707); DP 1003; EP 1394 (Ant); NP 1044
    [OOR 1831, Rd 1910f & 2043f; TD Pr 1149]

15. Wed. Easter Weekday or St. Isidore (1149)
    MP (1452) (588) 886; DP 1008; EP (1455) (590) 892; NP 1046
    [OOR 1835, Rd 1910f & 1989f or 2053f; Pr 1149 or 589]

16. Thu. Thursday of the 7th Week of Easter
    MP (591) 897; DP 1012; EP (592) 901; NP 1049
    [OOR 1838, Rd 1910f & 1989f; Pr 592]

17. Fri. Friday of the 7th Week of Easter
    MP (594) 906; DP 1017; EP (595) 911; NP 1052
    [OOR 1842, Rd 1910f & 1989f; Pr 595]

18. Sat. Easter Weekday or St. John I, Po & M (1150)
    MP (1414 or 1426) (597) 916; DP 1022
    EP 599; NP 1034
    [OOR 1845, Rd 1910f & 1989f or 2045f or 2046f; Pr 1150 or 598]

19. **Sun. PENTECOST (Sol) 603**
    MP 603 (707); DP 1027; EP 605; NP 1037
    [OOR 1850, Rd 1910f & 2008f; TD Pr 605]

20. Mon. The Blessed Virgin Mary, Mother of the Church (Mem) *(New)* Common of the Blessed Virgin Mary (1372)
    MP (1372) 867; DP 998; EP (1378) 872; NP 1041
    [OOR 1829, Rd 1924f & 1951f; Pr 39 in this Guide]

21. Tue. Weekday or St. Christopher Magallanes, P and Comps, Mm *(New)* (1402 or 1426)
    MP (1402 or 1426) 877; DP 1003
    EP (1405 or 1430) 882; NP 1044
    [OOR 1831, Rd 1924f & 2011f or 2045f; Pr 1404 or 1429 or 611]

22. Wed. Weekday or St. Rita of Cascia, Rel *(New)* (1462 & 1470)
MP (1463 & 1470) 886; DP 1008; EP (1466 & 1471) 892; NP 1046
[OOR 1835, Rd 1924f & 2011f or 2049f; Pr 1464 or 1471 or 611]

23. Thu. Thursday of the 7th Week in Ordinary Time
MP 897; DP 1012; EP 901; NP 1049
[OOR 1838, Rd 1924f & 2011f; Pr 611]

24. Fri. Friday of the 7th Week in Ordinary Time
MP 906; DP 1017; EP 911; NP 1052
[OOR 1842, Rd 1924f & 2011f; Pr 611]

25. Sat. Weekday or Venerable Bede, P & D (1151) or St. Gregory VII, Po
(1152) or St. Mary Magdalene de Pazzi, V (1152) or BVM on Saturday (1383)
MP (1434 or 1470) (1426) (1441 or 1470) (1383) 916; DP 1022
EP 641; NP 1034
[OOR 1845, Rd 1924f & 2046f or 2048f or 2049f or 1951f; Pr 1151 or
1152 or 1153 or 1386 or 611]

26. **Sun. TRINITY SUNDAY (Sol) 645**
MP 645 (707); DP 1027; EP 648; NP 1037
[OOR 1850, Rd 1924f & 2003f or 2009f; TD Pr 645]

27. Mon. Weekday or St. Augustine of Canterbury, B (1154)
MP (1426) 937; DP 998; EP (1430) 942; NP 1041
[OOR 1853, Rd 1924f & 2011f or 2046f; Pr 1154 or 612]

28. Tue. Tuesday of the 8th Week in Ordinary Time
MP 947; DP 1003; EP 953; NP 1044
[OOR 1856, Rd 1924f & 2011f; Pr 612]

29. Wed. Weekday or St. Paul VI, Po *(New)* (1426)
MP (1426) 958; DP 1008; EP (1430) 963; NP 1046
[OOR 1859, Rd 1924f & 2011f or 2046f; Pr 1428 or 612]

30. Thu. Thursday of the 8th Week in Ordinary Time
MP 968; DP 1012; EP 973; NP 1049
[OOR 1861, Rd 1924f & 2011f; Pr 612]

31. Fri. VISITATION OF MARY (F) 1154
MP 1154 (707); DP 1017; EP 1156 (1378); NP 1052
[OOR 1864; Rd 1924f & 1953f; TD Pr 1156]

JUNE

1. Sat. St. Justin, M (Mem) 1160
    MP (1414) (Ant) 988; DP 1022; EP 652; NP 1034
    [OOR 1867, Rd 1924f & 2045f; Pr 1160]

2. **Sun. CORPUS CHRISTI (Sol) 656**
    MP 656 (707); DP 1027; EP 658; NP 1037
    [OOR 1785, Rd 1924f & 2002f or 2011f; TD Pr 656]

3. Mon. Sts. Charles Lwanga and Comps, Mm (Mem) 1161
    MP (1402) 718; DP 998; EP (1405) 723; NP 1041
    [OOR 1788, Rd 1924f & 2045f; Pr 1162]

4. Tue. Tuesday of the 9th Week in Ordinary Time
    MP 728; DP 1003; EP 734; NP 1044
    [OOR 1791, Rd 1924f & 2011f; Pr 613]

5. Wed. St. Boniface, B & M (Mem) 1162
    MP (1414 or 1426) 738; DP 1008
    EP (1417 or 1430) 743; NP 1046
    [OOR 1794, Rd 1924f & 2045f; Pr 1162]

6. Thu. Weekday or St. Norbert, B (1163)
    MP (1426) 748; DP 1012; EP 663; NP 1034
    [OOR 1797, Rd 1924f & 2011f or 2046f; Pr 1163 or 613]

7. Fri. SACRED HEART (Sol) 667
    MP 667 (707); DP 1027; EP 669; NP 1037
    [OOR 1800, Rd 1924f & 2012f; TD Pr 666]

8. Sat. Immaculate Heart of Mary (Mem) (1159)
    MP (1372) (Ant) 770; DP 1022; EP 775 (614); NP 1034
    [OOR 1802, Rd 1924f & 1951f; Pr 1159]

9. **Sun. TENTH SUNDAY IN ORDINARY TIME 614**
    MP 780; DP 994; EP 786; NP 1037
    [OOR 1806, Rd 1924f & 2011f; TD Pr 614]

10. Mon. Monday of the 10th Week in Ordinary Time
    MP 792; DP 998; EP 798; NP 1041
    [OOR 1809, Rd 1924f & 2011f; Pr 614]

11. Tue. St. Barnabas, Ap (Mem) 1164
    MP (1165) 802; DP 1003; EP (1166) 807; NP 1044
    [OOR 1812, Rd 1924f & 2043f; Pr 1166]

12. Wed. Wednesday of the 10th Week in Ordinary Time
    MP 812; DP 1008; EP 818; NP 1046
    [OOR 1816, Rd 1924f & 2011f; Pr 614]

13. Thu. St. Anthony of Padua, P & D (Mem) 1168
    MP (1426 or 1435 or 1470) 824; DP 1012
    EP (1430 or 1436 or 1471) 830; NP 1049
    [OOR 1819, Rd 1924f & 2046f; Pr 1168]

14. Fri. Friday of the 10th Week in Ordinary Time
    MP 835; DP 1017; EP 840; NP 1052
    [OOR 1821, Rd 1924f & 2011f; Pr 614]

15. Sat. Weekday or BVM on Saturday (1383)
    MP (1383) 845; DP 1022; EP 851 (615); NP 1034
    [OOR 1824, Rd 1924f & 2011f or 1951f; Pr 1386 or 614]

16. **Sun. ELEVENTH SUNDAY IN ORDINARY TIME 615**
    MP 856; DP 994; EP 861; NP 1037
    [OOR 1827, Rd 1924f & 2011f; TD Pr 615]

17. Mon. Monday of the 11th Week in Ordinary Time
    MP 867; DP 998; EP 872; NP 1041
    [OOR 1829, Rd 1924f & 2011f; Pr 615]

18. Tue. Tuesday of the 11th Week in Ordinary Time
    MP 877; DP 1003; EP 882; NP 1044
    [OOR 1831, Rd 1924f & 2011f; Pr 615]

19. Wed. Weekday or St. Romuald, Ab (1169)
    MP (1470) 886; DP 1008; EP (1471) 892; NP 1046
    [OOR 1835, Rd 1924f & 2011f or 2049f; Pr 1169 or 615]

20. Thu. Thursday of the 11th Week in Ordinary Time
    MP 897; DP 1012; EP 901; NP 1049
    [OOR 1838, Rd 1924f & 2011f; Pr 615]

21. Fri. St. Aloysius Gonzaga, Rel (Mem) 1169
    MP (1470) 906; DP 1017; EP (1471) 911; NP 1052
    [OOR 1842, Rd 1924f & 2049f; Pr 1170]

22. Sat. Weekday or St. Paulinus of Nola, B (1170) or Sts. John Fisher, B & M,
    and Thomas More, M (1171) or BVM on Saturday (1383)
    MP (1426) (1402) (1383) 916; DP 1022; EP 921 (616); NP 1034
    [OOR 1845, Rd 1924f & 2011f or 2045f or 2046f or 1951f; Pr 1170 or
    1171 or 1386 or 615]

23.   **Sun. TWELFTH SUNDAY IN ORDINARY TIME 616**
MP 925; DP 994; EP 1172 (1448); NP 1034
[OOR 1850, Rd 1924f & 2011f; TD Pr 616]

24.   Mon. BIRTH OF ST. JOHN THE BAPTIST (Sol) 1174
MP 1174 (707); DP 1027; EP 1176 (1456); NP 1037
[OOR 1853, Rd 1924f & 1948f; TD Pr 1173]

25.   Tue. Tuesday of the 12th Week in Ordinary Time
MP 947; DP 1003; EP 953; NP 1044
[OOR 1856, Rd 1924f & 2011f; Pr 616]

26.   Wed. Wednesday of the 12th Week in Ordinary Time
MP 958; DP 1008; EP 963; NP 1046
[OOR 1859, Rd 1924f & 2011f; Pr 616]

27.   Thu. Weekday or St. Cyril of Alexandria, B & D (1178)
MP (1426 or 1435) 968; DP 1012
EP (1430 or 1436) 973; NP 1049
[OOR 1861, Rd 1924f & 2011f or 2046f; Pr 1178 or 616]

28.   Fri. St. Irenaeus, B & M (Mem) 1178
MP (1414 or 1426) (Ant) 978; DP 1017; EP 1179 (1389); NP 1034
[OOR 1864, Rd 1924f & 2045f; Pr 1179]

29.   Sat. STS. PETER AND PAUL, AP (Sol) 1181
MP 1181 (707); DP 1027; EP 1183 (1394); NP 1037
[OOR 1867, Rd 1924f & 2043f; TD Pr 1183]

30.   **Sun. THIRTEENTH SUNDAY IN ORDINARY TIME 617**
MP 706; DP 994; EP 712; NP 1037
[OOR 1785, Rd 1924f & 2011f; TD Pr 617]

JULY

1.   Mon. Weekday or St. Junipero Serra, P **(New)** (8)
MP (1426 or 1470) 718, Pr (8) or 1429; DP 998
EP (1430 or 1471) 723, Pr (8) or 1429; NP 1041
[OOR 1788, Rd 1924f & 2011f or 2046f; Pr (8) or 1429 or 617]

2.   Tue. Tuesday of the 13th Week in Ordinary Time
MP 728; DP 1003; EP 734; NP 1044
[OOR 1791, Rd 1924f & 2011f; Pr 617]

3. Wed. ST. THOMAS, AP (F) 1186
    MP 1187 (707); DP 1008; EP 1188 (1394); NP 1046
    [OOR 1794, Rd 1924f & 2043f; TD Pr 1188]

4. Thu. Thursday of the 13th Week in Ordinary Time
    MP 748; DP 1012; EP 754; NP 1049
    [OOR 1797, Rd 1924f & 2011f; Pr 617]

5. Fri. Weekday or St. Anthony Zaccaria, P (1190) or St. Elizabeth of
        Portugal (1189) **[transferred from 7/4]**
    MP (1426 or 1473 or 1470) (1472) 759; DP 1017
    EP (1430 or 1473 or 1471) (1472) 765; NP 1052
    [OOR 1800, Rd 1924f & 2011f or 2046f or 2053f; Pr 1190 or 1189 or 617]

6. Sat. Weekday or St. Maria Goretti, V & M (1190) or BVM on Saturday (1383)
    MP (1414 or 1441) (1383) 770; DP 1022; EP (618) 775; NP 1034
    [OOR 1802, Rd 1924f & 2011f or 2045f or 1951f; Pr 1190 or 1386 or 617]

7. **Sun. FOURTEENTH SUNDAY IN ORDINARY TIME 618**
    MP 780; DP 994; EP 786; NP 1037
    [OOR 1806, Rd 1924f & 2011f; TD Pr 618]

8. Mon. Monday of the 14th Week in Ordinary Time
    MP 792; DP 998; EP 798; NP 1041
    [OOR 1809, Rd 1924f & 2011f; Pr 618]

9. Tue. Weekday or St. Augustine Zhao Rong, P, and Comps, Mm *(New)*
        (1402 or 1426)
    MP (1402 or 1426) 802; DP 1003; EP (1405 or 1430) 807; NP 1044
    [OOR 1812, Rd 1924f & 2011f or 2045f; Pr 1404 or 1429 or 618]

10. Wed. Wednesday of the 14th Week in Ordinary Time
    MP 812; DP 1008; EP 818; NP 1046
    [OOR 1816, Rd 1924f & 2011f; Pr 618]

11. Thu. St. Benedict, Ab (Mem) 1191
    MP (1470) (Ant) 824; DP 1012; EP (1471) (Ant) 830; NP 1049
    [OOR 1819, Rd 1924f & 2049f; Pr 1191]

12. Fri. Friday of the 14th Week in Ordinary Time
    MP 835; DP 1017; EP 840; NP 1052
    [OOR 1821, Rd 1924f & 2011f; Pr 618]

13. Sat. Weekday or St. Henry (1192) or BVM on Saturday (1383)
    MP (1452) (1383) 845; DP 1022; EP 851 (619); NP 1034
    [OOR 1824, Rd 1924f & 2011f or 2053f or 1951f; Pr 1192 or 1386 or 618]

14. **Sun. FIFTEENTH SUNDAY IN ORDINARY TIME 619**
    MP 856; DP 994; EP 861; NP 1037
    [OOR 1827, Rd 1924f & 2011f; TD Pr 619]

15. Mon. St. Bonaventure, B & D (Mem) 1193
    MP (1426 or 1435) 867; DP 998; EP (1430 or 1436) 872; NP 1041
    [OOR 1829, Rd 1924f & 2046f; Pr 1194]

16. Tue. Weekday or Our Lady of Mount Carmel (1194)
    MP (1372) (Ant) 877; DP 1003; EP (1378) (Ant) 882; NP 1044
    [OOR 1831, Rd 1924f & 2011f or 1951f; Pr 1194 or 619]

17. Wed. Wednesday of the 15th Week in Ordinary Time
    MP 886; DP 1008; EP 892; NP 1046
    [OOR 1835, Rd 1924f & 2011f; Pr 619]

18. Thu. Weekday or St. Camillus de Lellis, P (1193) **[transferred from 7/14]**
    MP (1472) 897; DP 1012; EP (1472) 901; NP 1049
    [OOR 1838, Rd 1924f & 2011f or 2046f; Pr 1193 or 619]

19. Fri. Friday of the 15th Week in Ordinary Time
    MP 906; DP 1017; EP 911; NP 1052
    [OOR 1842, Rd 1924f & 2011f; Pr 619]

20. Sat. Weekday or St. Apollinaris, B & M *(New)* (1414 or 1426) or BVM on
    Saturday (1383)
    MP (1414 or 1426) (1383) 916; DP 1022; EP 921 (620); NP 1034
    [OOR 1845, Rd 1924f & 2011f or 2045f or 2046f or 1951f; Pr 1416 or
    1428 or 1386 or 619]

21. **Sun. SIXTEENTH SUNDAY IN ORDINARY TIME 620**
    MP 925; DP 994; EP 931; NP 1037
    [OOR 1850, Rd 1924f & 2011f; TD Pr 620]

22. Mon. ST. MARY MAGDALENE (F) 1195
    MP 1196 (707); DP 998; EP 1197 (1466); NP 1041
    [OOR 1853, Rd 1924f & 2053f; Pr 1197]

23. Tue. Weekday or St. Bridget, Rel (1198)
    MP (1470) 947; DP 1003; EP (1471) 953; NP 1044
    [OOR 1856, Rd 1924f & 2011f or 2049f; Pr 1198 or 620]

24. Wed. Weekday or St. Sharbel Makhlūf, P *(New)* (1426)
    MP (1426 or 1470) 958; DP 1008; EP (1430 or 1471) 963; NP 1046
    [OOR 1859, Rd 1924f & 2011f or 2046f; Pr 1429 or 620]

25.　Thu. ST. JAMES, AP (F) 1199
　　MP 1199 (707); DP 1012; EP 1200 (1394); NP 1049
　　[OOR 1861, Rd 1924f & 2043f; TD Pr 1200]

26.　Fri. Sts. Joachim and Ann, Parents of Mary (Mem) 1201
　　MP 1202 (978); DP 1017; EP 1203 (984); NP 1052
　　[OOR 1864, Rd 1924f & 2053f; Pr 1202]

27.　Sat. Weekday or BVM on Saturday (1383)
　　MP (1383) 988; DP 1022; EP (621) 701; NP 1034
　　[OOR 1867, Rd 1924f & 2011f or 1951f; Pr 1386 or 620]

28.　**Sun. SEVENTEENTH SUNDAY IN ORDINARY TIME 621**
　　MP 706; DP 994; EP 712; NP 1037
　　[OOR 1785, Rd 1924f & 2011f; TD Pr 621]

29.　Mon. Sts. Martha, Mary and Lazarus (Mem) *(New)*
　　MP (1452) 718; DP 998; EP (1455) 723; NP 1041
　　[OOR 1788, Rd 1924f & 2053f; Pr 1454]

30.　Tue. Weekday or St. Peter Chrysologus, B & D (1204)
　　MP (1426 or 1435) 728; DP 1003; EP (1430 or 1436) 734; NP 1044
　　[OOR 1791, Rd 1924f & 2011f or 2046f; Pr 1205 or 621]

31.　Wed. St. Ignatius of Loyola, P (Mem) 1205
　　MP (1426 or 1470) (Ant) 738; DP 1008
　　EP (1430 or 1471) (Ant) 743; NP 1046
　　[OOR 1794, Rd 1924f & 2046f; Pr 1206]

AUGUST

1.　Thu. St. Alphonsus Liguori, B & D (Mem) 1206
　　MP (1426 or 1435) 748; DP 1012; EP (1430 or 1436) 754; NP 1049
　　[OOR 1797, Rd 1924f & 2046f; Pr 1207]

2.　Fri. Weekday or St. Eusebius of Vercelli, B (1207) or St. Peter Julian
　　　　Eymard, P *(New)* (1426 or 1470)
　　MP (1426) (1426 or 1470) 759; DP 1017
　　EP (1430) (1430 or 1471) 765; NP 1052
　　[OOR 1800, Rd 1924f & 2011f or 2046f; Pr 1207 or 1429 or 1471 or 621]

3.　Sat. Weekday or BVM on Saturday (1383)
　　MP (1383) 770; DP 1022; EP (622) 775; NP 1034
　　[OOR 1802, Rd 1924f & 2011f or 1951f; Pr 1386 or 621]

4. **Sun. EIGHTEENTH SUNDAY IN ORDINARY TIME 622**
MP 780; DP 994; EP 786; NP 1037
[OOR 1806, Rd 1924f & 2011f; TD Pr 622]

5. Mon. Weekday or Dedication of St. Mary Major (1208)
MP (1372) (Ant) 792; DP 998; EP (1378) 798; NP 1041
[OOR 1809, Rd 1924f & 2011f or 1951f; Pr 1209 or 622]

6. Tue. TRANSFIGURATION OF OUR LORD (F) 1213
MP 1213 (707); DP 1003; EP 1215; NP 1044
[OOR 1812, Rd 1924f & 1977f; TD Pr 1215]

7. Wed. Weekday or St. Sixtus II, Po & M and Comps, Mm (1219) or St.
Cajetan, P (1220)
MP (1402) (1426 or 1470) 812; DP 1008
EP (1405) (1430 or 1471) 818; NP 1046
[OOR 1816, Rd 1924f & 2011f or 2045f or 2049f or 2046f; Pr 1219 or
1220 or 622]

8. Thu. St. Dominic, P (Mem) 1220
MP (1426 or 1470) 824; DP 1012; EP (1430 or 1471) 830; NP 1049
[OOR 1819, Rd 1924f & 2046f or 2049f; Pr 1221]

9. Fri. Weekday or St. Teresa Benedicta of the Cross, V & M (Edith Stein)
(New) (1414 or 1441)
MP (1414 or 1441) 835; DP 1017; EP (1417 or 1444) 840; NP 1052
[OOR 1821, Rd 1924f & 2011f or 2045f or 2048f; Pr 1417 or 1443 or 622]

10. Sat. ST. LAWRENCE, DE & M (F) 1221
MP 1221 (707); DP 1022; EP 851 (623); NP 1034
[OOR 1824, Rd 1924f & 2045f; TD Pr 1222]

11. **Sun. NINETEENTH SUNDAY IN ORDINARY TIME 623**
MP 856; DP 994; EP 861; NP 1037
[OOR 1827, Rd 1924f & 2011f; TD Pr 624]

12. Mon. Weekday or St. Jane Frances de Chantal, Rel (1340) or **(New)**
(14) [Transferred from 8/18]
MP (1470) 867; DP 998; EP (1471) 872; NP 1041
[OOR 1829, Rd 1924f & 2011f or 2016f; Pr 1340 or (17) or 624]

13. Tue. Weekday or Sts. Pontian, Po & M, and Hippolytus, P & M (1224)
MP (1402 or 1426) 877; DP 1003; EP (1405 or 1430) 882; NP 1044
[OOR 1831, Rd 1924f & 2011f or 2045f; Pr 1225 or 624]

14.   Wed. St. Maximilian Kolbe, P & M (Mem) **(New)** (10)
      MP (1414 or 1426) (Ant & Pr proper [14]) 886; DP 1008
      EP 1225 (1368); NP 1034
      [OOR 1835, Rd 1924f & 2045f; Pr proper (13) or 1416 or 1429 (Miss)]

15.   **Thu. ASSUMPTION (Sol) 1227**
      MP 1227 (707); DP 1027; EP 1229 (1378); NP 1037
      [OOR 1838, Rd 1924f & 1951f; TD Pr 1229]

16.   Fri. Weekday or St. Stephen of Hungary (1231)
      MP (1452) 906; DP 1017; EP (1455) 911; NP 1052
      [OOR 1842, Rd 1924f & 2053f; Pr 1231 or 624]

17.   Sat. Weekday or BVM on Saturday (1383)
      MP (1383) 916; DP 1022; EP (624) 921; NP 1034
      [OOR 1845, Rd 1924f & 2011f or 1951f; Pr 1386 or 624]

18.   **Sun. TWENTIETH SUNDAY IN ORDINARY TIME 624**
      MP 925; DP 994; EP 931; NP 1037
      [OOR 1850, Rd 1924f & 2011f; TD Pr 625]

19.   Mon. Weekday or St. John Eudes, P (1232)
      MP (1426 or 1470) 937; DP 998; EP (1430 or 1471) 942; NP 1041
      [OOR 1853, Rd 1924f & 2011f or 2046f; Pr 1232 or 625]

20.   Tue. St. Bernard, Ab & D (Mem) 1232
      MP (1435 or 1470) (Ant) 947; DP 1003
      EP (1436 or 1471) (Ant) 953; NP 1044
      [OOR 1856, Rd 1924f & 2049f; Pr 1233]

21.   Wed. St. Pius X, Po (Mem) 1233
      MP (1426) 958; DP 1008; EP (1430) 963; NP 1046
      [OOR 1859, Rd 1924f & 2046f; Pr 1234]

22.   Thu. Queenship of Mary (Mem) 1234
      MP (1372) (Ant) 968; DP 1012; EP (1378) (Ant) 973; NP 1049
      [OOR 1861, Rd 1924f & 1951f; Pr 1234]

23.   Fri. Weekday or St. Rose of Lima, V (1235)
      MP (1441 or 1470) 978; DP 1017; EP (1444 or 1471) 984; NP 1052
      [OOR 1864, Rd 1924f & 2011f or 2048f; Pr 1235 or 625]

24.   Sat. ST. BARTHOLOMEW, AP (F) 1236
      MP 1392 (707); DP 1022; EP 701 (626); NP 1034
      [OOR 1867, Rd 1924f & 2043f; TD Pr 1236]

25. **Sun. TWENTY-FIRST SUNDAY IN ORDINARY TIME 626**
MP 706; DP 994; EP 712; NP 1037
[OOR 1785, Rd 1924f & 2011f; TD Pr 626]

26. Mon. Monday of the 21st Week in Ordinary Time
MP 718; DP 998; EP 723; NP 1041
[OOR 1788, Rd 1924f & 2011f; Pr 626]

27. Tue. St. Monica (Mem) 1238
MP (1463) (Ant) 728; DP 1003; EP (1466) (Ant) 734; NP 1044
[OOR 1791, Rd 1924f & 2053f; Pr 1238]

28. Wed. St. Augustine, B & D (Mem) 1239
MP (1426 or 1435) (Ant) 738; DP 1008
EP (1430 or 1436) (Ant) 743; NP 1046
[OOR 1794, Rd 1924f & 2046f; Pr 1239]

29. Thu. Beheading of St. John the Baptist, M (Mem) 1240
MP 1240 (707); DP 1012; EP 1242 (1417); NP 1049
[OOR 1797, Rd 1924f & 2045f; Pr 1241]

30. Fri. Friday of the 21st Week in Ordinary Time
MP 759; DP 1017; EP 765; NP 1052
[OOR 1800, Rd 1924f & 2011f; Pr 626]

31. Sat. Weekday or BVM on Saturday (1383)
MP (1383) 770; DP 1022; EP (627) 775; NP 1034
[OOR 1802, Rd 1924f & 2011f or 1951f; Pr 1386 or 626]

SEPTEMBER

1. **Sun. TWENTY-SECOND SUNDAY IN ORDINARY TIME 627**
MP 780; DP 994; EP 786; NP 1037
[OOR 1806, Rd 1924f & 2011f; TD Pr 627]

2. Mon. Monday of the 22nd Week in Ordinary Time
MP 792; DP 998; EP 798; NP 1041
[OOR 1809, Rd 1924f & 2011f; Pr 627]

3. Tue. St. Gregory the Great, Po & D (Mem) 1244
MP (1426 or 1435) (Ant) 802; DP 1003
EP (1430 or 1436) (Ant) 807; NP 1044
[OOR 1812, Rd 1924f & 2046f; Pr 1244]

4. Wed. Wednesday of the 22nd Week in Ordinary Time
    MP 812; DP 1008; EP 818; NP 1046
    [OOR 1816, Rd 1924f & 2011f; Pr 627]

5. Thu. Thursday of the 22nd Week in Ordinary Time
    MP 824; DP 1012; EP 830; NP 1049
    [OOR 1819, Rd 1924f & 2011f; Pr 627]

6. Fri. Friday of the 22nd Week in Ordinary Time
    MP 835; DP 1017; EP 840; NP 1052
    [OOR 1821, Rd 1924f & 2011f; Pr 627]

7. Sat. Weekday or BVM on Saturday (1383)
    MP (1383) 845; DP 1022; EP (628) 851; NP 1034
    [OOR 1824, Rd 1924f & 2011f or 1951f; Pr 1386 or 627]

8. **Sun. TWENTY-THIRD SUNDAY IN ORDINARY TIME 628**
    MP 856; DP 994; EP 861; NP 1037
    [OOR 1827, Rd 1924f & 2011f; TD Pr 628]

9. Mon. St. Peter Claver, P (Mem) 1248
    MP (1426 or 1472) 867; DP 998
    EP (1430 or 1472) 872; NP 1041
    [OOR 1829, Rd 1924f & 2046f; Pr 1249]

10. Tue. Tuesday of the 23rd Week in Ordinary Time
    MP 877; DP 1003; EP 882; NP 1044
    [OOR 1831, Rd 1924f & 2011f; Pr 628]

11. Wed. Wednesday of the 23rd Week in Ordinary Time
    MP 886; DP 1008; EP 892; NP 1046
    [OOR 1835, Rd 1924f & 2011f; Pr 628]

12. Thu. Weekday or Most Holy Name of Mary *(New)* Common of the
    Blessed Virgin Mary (1372)
    MP (1372) (Ant) 897; DP 1012; EP (1378) 901; NP 1049
    [OOR 1838, Rd 1924f & 2011f or 1951f; Pr 1376f or 628]

13. Fri. St. John Chrysostom, B & D (Mem) 1249
    MP (1426 or 1435) 906; DP 1017; EP (1430 or 1436) 911; NP 1052
    [OOR 1842, Rd 1924f & 2046f, Pr 1250]

14. Sat. TRIUMPH OF THE CROSS (F) 1254
    MP 1254 (707); DP 1022; EP (629) 921; NP 1034
    [OOR 1845, Rd 1924f & 1984f; TD Pr 1254]

15. **Sun. TWENTY-FOURTH SUNDAY IN ORDINARY TIME 629**
     MP 925; DP 994; EP 931; NP 1037
     [OOR 1850, Rd 1924f & 2011f; TD Pr 629]

16. Mon. Sts. Cornelius, Po & M and Cyprian, B & M (Mem) 1263
     MP (1402 or 1426) (Ant) 937; DP 998
     EP (1405 or 1430) (Ant) 942; NP 1041
     [OOR 1853, Rd 1924f & 2045f; Pr 1264]

17. Tue. Weekday or St. Robert Bellarmine, B & D (1265) or St. Hildegard
        of Bingen, V & D *(New)* (1441)
     MP (1426 or 1435) (1441 or 1470) 947; DP 1003
     EP (1430 or 1436) (1444 or 1471) 953; NP 1044
     [OOR 1856, Rd 1924f & 2011f or 2046f or 2048f or 2049f; Pr 1265 or
        1443 or 1471 or 629]

18. Wed. Wednesday of the 24th Week in Ordinary Time
     MP 958; DP 1008; EP 963; NP 1046
     [OOR 1859, Rd 1924f & 2011f; Pr 629]

19. Thu. Weekday or St. Januarius, B & M (1265)
     MP (1414 or 1426) 968; DP 1012; EP (1417 or 1430) 973; NP 1049
     [OOR 1861, Rd 1924f & 2011f or 2045f; Pr 1266 or 629]

20. Fri. Sts. Andrew Kim Tae-gŏn, P & M, Paul Chŏng Ha-sang, and Comps,
        Mm (Mem) **(New)** (17)
     MP (1402) 978, Pr proper (21); DP 1017; EP (1405) 984; NP 1052
     [OOR 1864, Rd 1924f & 2045f or proper (18); Pr proper (21) or 1404]

21. Sat. ST. MATTHEW, AP & EVANGELIST (F) 1266
     MP 1392 (707) (Ant); DP 1022; EP (630) 701; NP 1034
     [OOR 1867, Rd 1924f & 2043f; TD Pr 1266]

22. **Sun. TWENTY-FIFTH SUNDAY IN ORDINARY TIME 630**
     MP 706; DP 994; EP 712; NP 1037
     [OOR 1785, Rd 1924f & 2011f; TD Pr 631]

23. Mon. St. Pius of Pietrelcina, P (Mem) *(New)* (1426)
     MP (1426) 718; DP 998; EP (1430) 723; NP 1041
     [OOR 1788, Rd 1924f & 2046f; Pr 1429]

24. Tue. Tuesday of the 25th Week in Ordinary Time
     MP 728; DP 1003; EP 734; NP 1044
     [OOR 1791, Rd 1924f & 2011f; Pr 631]

25. Wed. Wednesday of the 25th Week in Ordinary Time
MP 738; DP 1008; EP 743; NP 1046
[OOR 1794, Rd 1924f & 2011f; Pr 631]

26. Thu. Weekday or Sts. Cosmas and Damian, Mm (1267)
MP (1402) 748; DP 1012; EP (1405) 754; NP 1049
[OOR 1797, Rd 1924f & 2045f; Pr 1267 or 631]

27. Fri. St. Vincent de Paul, P (Mem) 1267
MP (1426 or 1472) (Ant) 759; DP 1017
EP (1430 or 1472) (Ant) 765; NP 1052
[OOR 1800, Rd 1924f & 2046f; Pr 1268]

28. Sat. Weekday or St. Wenceslaus, M (1268) or St. Lawrence Ruiz and
Comps, Mm **(New)** (21) Pr proper (24) or 1404 or BVM on Saturday
(1383)
MP (1414) (1402) (1383) 770; DP 1022; EP 775 (631); NP 1034
[OOR 1802, Rd 1924f & 2011f or 2045f or proper (22); Pr 1269 or proper
(24) or 1404 or 1386 or 631]

29. **Sun. TWENTY-SIXTH SUNDAY IN ORDINARY TIME 632**
MP 780; DP 994; EP 786; NP 1037
[OOR 1806, Rd 1924f & 2011f; TD Pr 632]

30. Mon. St. Jerome, P & D (Mem) 1275
MP (1435) 792; DP 998; EP (1436) 798; NP 1041
[OOR 1809, Rd 1924f & 2046f; Pr 1275]

OCTOBER

1. Tue. St. Theresa of the Child Jesus, V & D (Mem) 1276
MP (1435 or 1441) (Ant) 802; DP 1003
EP (1436 or 1444) (Ant) 807; NP 1044
[OOR 1812, Rd 1924f & 2048f; Pr 1276]

2. Wed. Guardian Angels (Mem) 1277
MP 1277 (707); DP 1008; EP 1279; NP 1046
[OOR 1816, Rd 1924f & 2011f; Pr 1278]

3. Thu. Thursday of the 26th Week in Ordinary Time
MP 824; DP 1012; EP 830; NP 1049
[OOR 1819, Rd 1924f & 2011f; Pr 632]

4. Fri. St. Francis of Assisi (Mem) 1283
MP (1470) (Ant) 835; DP 1017; EP (1471) (Ant) 840; NP 1052
[OOR 1821, Rd 1924f & 2049f; Pr 1283]

5. Sat. Weekday or St. Faustina Kowalska, V *(New)* (1441 or 1470) or Bl. Francis Xavier Seelos, P *(New)* (1426) or BVM on Saturday (1383)
MP (1441 or 1470) (1426) (1383) 845; DP 1022; EP (633) 851; NP 1034
[OOR 1824, Rd 1924f & 2011f or 2048f or 2046f or 1951f; Pr 1443 or 1471 or 1429 or 1386 or 632]

6. **Sun. TWENTY-SEVENTH SUNDAY IN ORDINARY TIME 633**
MP 856; DP 994; EP 861; NP 1037
[OOR 1827, Rd 1924f & 2011f; TD Pr 633]

7. Mon. Our Lady of the Rosary (Mem) 1284
MP 1285 (707); DP 998; EP 1286 (1378); NP 1041
[OOR 1829, Rd 1924f & 1951f; Pr 1286]

8. Tue. Tuesday of the 27th Week in Ordinary Time
MP 877; DP 1003; EP 882; NP 1044
[OOR 1831, Rd 1924f & 2011f; Pr 633]

9. Wed. Weekday or St. Denis, B & M, and Comps, Mm (1287) or St. John Leonardi, P (1288)
MP (1402) (1426 or 1472) 886; DP 1008
EP (1405) (1430 or 1472) 892; NP 1046
[OOR 1835, Rd 1924f & 2011f or 2045f or 2046f or 2049f; Pr 1287 or 1288 or 633]

10. Thu. Thursday of the 27th Week in Ordinary Time
MP 897; DP 1012; EP 901; NP 1049
[OOR 1838, Rd 1924f & 2011f; Pr 633]

11. Fri. Weekday or St. John XXIII, Po *(New)* (1426)
MP (1426) 906; DP 1017; EP (1430) 911; NP 1052
[OOR 1842, Rd 1924f & 2011f or 2046f; Pr 1428 or 633]

12. Sat. Weekday or BVM on Saturday (1383)
MP (1383) 916; DP 1022; EP (634) 921; NP 1034
[OOR 1845, Rd 1924f & 2011f or 1951f; Pr 1386 or 633]

13. **Sun. TWENTY-EIGHTH SUNDAY IN ORDINARY TIME 634**
MP 925; DP 994; EP 931; NP 1037
[OOR 1850, Rd 1924f & 2011f; TD Pr 634]

14. Mon. Weekday or St. Callistus I, Po & M (1289)
MP (1414 or 1426) 937; DP 998; EP (1417 or 1430) 942; NP 1041
[OOR 1853, Rd 1924f & 2011f or 2045f; Pr 1289 or 634)

15. Tue. St. Teresa of Avila, V & D (Mem) 1289
MP (1435 or 1441) 947; DP 1003
EP (1436 or 1444) 953; NP 1044
[OOR 1856, Rd 1924f & 2048f; Pr 1290]

16. Wed. Weekday or St. Hedwig, Rel (1290) or St. Margaret Mary Alacoque,
V (1290)
MP (1472 or 1470) (1441 or 1470) 958; DP 1008
EP (1472 or 1471) (1444 or 1471) 963; NP 1046
[OOR 1859, Rd 1924f & 2048f or 2049f; Pr 1290 or 1291 or 634]

17. Thu. St. Ignatius of Antioch, B & M (Mem) 1291
MP (1414 or 1426) (Ant) 968; DP 1012
EP (1417 or 1430) (Ant) 973; NP 1049
[OOR 1861, Rd 1924f & 2045f; Pr 1292]

18. Fri. ST. LUKE, EVANGELIST (F) 1292
MP 1293 (707); DP 1017; EP 1295 (1394); NP 1052
[OOR 1864, Rd 1924f & 2043f; TD Pr 1294]

19. Sat. Sts. Isaac Jogues and John de Brébeuf, Pp & Mm, and Comps,
Mm (Mem) 1297
MP (1402 or 1426) 988; DP 1022; EP 701 (635); NP 1034
[OOR 1867, Rd 1924f & 2045f; Pr 1297]

20. **Sun. TWENTY-NINTH SUNDAY IN ORDINARY TIME 635**
MP 706; DP 994; EP 712; NP 1037
[OOR 1785, Rd 1924f & 2011f; TD Pr 635]

21. Mon. Monday of the 29th Week in Ordinary Time
MP 718; DP 998; EP 723; NP 1041
[OOR 1788, Rd 1924f & 2011f; Pr 635]

22. Tue. Weekday or St. John Paul II, Po *(New)* (1426)
MP (1426) 728; DP 1003; EP (1430) 734; NP 1044
[OOR 1791, Rd 1924f & 2011f or 2046f; Pr 1428 or 635]

23. Wed. Weekday or St. John Capistrano, P (1298)
MP (1426) 738; DP 1008; EP (1430) 743; NP 1046
[OOR 1794, Rd 1924f & 2011f or 2046f; Pr 1298 or 635]

24.   Thu. Weekday or St. Anthony Claret, B (1299)
MP (1426) 748; DP 1012; EP (1430) 754; NP 1049
[OOR 1797, Rd 1924f & 2011f or 2046f; Pr 1299 or 635]

25.   Fri. Friday of the 29th Week in Ordinary Time
MP 759; DP 1017; EP 765; NP 1052
[OOR 1800, Rd 1924f & 2011f; Pr 635]

26.   Sat. Weekday or BVM on Saturday (1383)
MP (1383) 770; DP 1022; EP (636) 775; NP 1034
[OOR 1802, Rd 1924f & 2011f or 1951f; Pr 1386 or 635]

27.   **Sun. THIRTIETH SUNDAY IN ORDINARY TIME 636**
MP 780; DP 994; EP 786; NP 1037
[OOR 1806, Rd 1924f & 2011f; TD Pr 636]

28.   Mon. STS. SIMON AND JUDE, AP (F) 1299
MP 1392 (707); DP 998; EP 1394; NP 1041
[OOR 1809, Rd 1924f & 2043f; TD Pr 1300]

29.   Tue. Tuesday of the 30th Week in Ordinary Time
MP 802; DP 1003; EP 807; NP 1044
[OOR 1812, Rd 1924f & 2011f; Pr 636]

30.   Wed. Wednesday of the 30th Week in Ordinary Time
MP 812; DP 1008; EP 818; NP 1046
[OOR 1816, Rd 1924f & 2011f; Pr 636]

31.   Thu. Thursday of the 30th Week in Ordinary Time
MP 824; DP 1012; EP 1300; NP 1034
[OOR 1819, Rd 1924f & 2011f; Pr 636]

NOVEMBER

1.   **Fri. ALL SAINTS (Sol) 1304**
MP 1304 (707); DP 1027; EP 1306; NP 1037
[OOR 1821, Rd 1924f & 2036f or 2053f; TD Pr 1304]

2.   Sat. ALL SOULS 1310
MP 1486; DP 1493; EP (637) 851; NP 1034
[OOR 1474, Rd 1478f & 2034f; Pr 1310]

3.   **Sun. THIRTY-FIRST SUNDAY IN ORDINARY TIME 637**
MP 856; DP 994; EP 861; NP 1037
[OOR 1827, Rd 1924f & 2011f; TD Pr 637]

4. Mon. St. Charles Borromeo, B (Mem) 1311
    MP (1426) 867; DP 998; EP (1430) 872; NP 1041
    [OOR 1829, Rd 1924f & 2046f; Pr 1312]

5. Tue. Tuesday of the 31st Week in Ordinary Time
    MP 877; DP 1003; EP 882; NP 1044
    [OOR 1831, Rd 1924f & 2011f; Pr 637]

6. Wed. Wednesday of the 31st Week in Ordinary Time
    MP 886; DP 1008; EP 892; NP 1046
    [OOR 1835, Rd 1924f & 2011f; Pr 637]

7. Thu. Thursday of the 31st Week in Ordinary Time
    MP 897; DP 1012; EP 901; NP 1049
    [OOR 1838, Rd 1924f & 2011f; Pr 637]

8. Fri. Friday of the 31st Week in Ordinary Time
    MP 906; DP 1017; EP 911; NP 1052
    [OOR 1842, Rd 1924f & 2011f; Pr 637]

9. Sat. DEDICATION OF ST. JOHN LATERAN (F) 1312
    MP 1360 (707); DP 1022; EP (638) 921; NP 1034
    [OOR 1845, Rd 1924f & 2011f; TD Pr 1362]

10. Sun. **THIRTY-SECOND SUNDAY IN ORDINARY TIME 638**
    MP 925; DP 994; EP 931; NP 1037
    [OOR 1850, Rd 1924f & 2011f; TD Pr 638]

11. Mon. St. Martin of Tours, B (Mem) 1313
    MP 1314 (707); DP 998; EP 1315 (1430); NP 1041
    [OOR 1853, Rd 1924f & 2046f; Pr 1315]

12. Tue. St. Josaphat, B & M (Mem) 1316
    MP (1414 or 1426) 947; DP 1003
    EP (1417 or 1430) 953; NP 1044
    [OOR 1856, Rd 1924f & 2045f; Pr 1317]

13. Wed. St. Frances Xavier Cabrini, V (Mem) 1317
    MP (1441 or 1470 or 1472) 958; DP 1008
    EP (1444 or 1471 or 1472) 963; NP 1046
    [OOR 1859, Rd 1924f & 2048f; Pr 1318]

14. Thu. Thursday of the 32nd Week in Ordinary Time
    MP 968; DP 1012; EP 973; NP 1049
    [OOR 1861, Rd 1924f & 2011f; Pr 638]

15.   Fri. Weekday or St. Albert the Great, B & D (1318)
      MP (1426 or 1435) 978; DP 1017; EP (1430 or 1436) 984; NP 1052
      [OOR 1864, Rd 1924f & 2011f or 2046f; Pr 1318 or 638]

16.   Sat. Weekday or St. Margaret of Scotland (1319) or St. Gertrude, V
            (1319) or BVM on Saturday (1383)
      MP (1472) (1441 or 1470) (1383) 988; DP 1022
      EP 701 (639); NP 1034
      [OOR 1867, Rd 1924f & 2011f or 2053f or 2048f or 1951f; Pr 1319 or
            1320 or 1386 or 638]

17.   **Sun. THIRTY-THIRD SUNDAY IN ORDINARY TIME 639**
      MP 706; DP 994; EP 712; NP 1037
      [OOR 1785, Rd 1924f & 2011f; TD Pr 640]

18.   Mon. Weekday or Dedication of the Churches of Sts. Peter and Paul, Ap
            (1321) or St. Rose Philippine Duchesne, V **(New)** (26)
      MP (1392) (1441) (Ant) 718; DP 998; Pr 1321 or (27) or 1443
      EP (1394) (1444) (Ant) 723; NP 1041
      [OOR 1788, Rd 1924f & 2011f or 2043f or 2048f; Pr 1321 or (27) or 1443
            or 640]

19.   Tue. Tuesday of the 33rd Week in Ordinary Time
      MP 728; DP 1003; EP 734; NP 1044
      [OOR 1791, Rd 1924f & 2011f; Pr 640]

20.   Wed. Wednesday of the 33rd Week in Ordinary Time
      MP 738; DP 1008; EP 743; NP 1046
      [OOR 1794, Rd 1924f & 2011f; Pr 640]

21.   Thu. Presentation of Mary (Mem) 1322
      MP (1372) (Ant) 748; DP 1012; EP (1378) (Ant) 754; NP 1049
      [OOR 1797, Rd 1924f & 1951f; Pr 1322]

22.   Fri. St. Cecilia, V & M (Mem) 1323
      MP (1414 or 1441) (Ant) 759; DP 1017
      EP (1417 or 1444) (Ant) 765; NP 1052
      [OOR 1800, Rd 1924f & 2045f or 2048f; Pr 1323]

23.   Sat. Weekday or St. Clement I, Po & M (1324) or St. Columban,
            Ab (1324) or Bl. Miguel Agustín Pro, P & M **(New)** (27) or BVM on
            Saturday (1383)
      MP (1414 or 1426) (1426 or 1470) (1383) 770; DP 1022
      EP 674; NP 1034

[OOR 1802, Rd 1924f & 2011f or 2045f or 2046f or 2049f or 1951f; Pr 1324 or 1325 or (28) or 1416 or 1429 or 1386 or 640]

24. **Sun. CHRIST THE KING (Sol) 677**
MP 677 (707); DP 1027; EP 679; NP 1037
[OOR 1806, Rd 1924f & 2011f; TD Pr 677]

25. Mon. Weekday or St. Catherine of Alexandria, V & M *(New)* (1414 or 1441)
MP (1414 or 1441) 792; DP 998; EP (1417 or 1444) 798; NP 1041
[OOR 1809, Rd 1924f & 2011f or 2045f or 2048f; Pr 1417 or 1443 or 640]

26. Tue. Tuesday of the 34th Week in Ordinary Time
MP 802; DP 1003; EP 807; NP 1044
[OOR 1812, Rd 1924f & 2011f; Pr 640]

27. Wed. Wednesday of the 34th Week in Ordinary Time
MP 812; DP 1008; EP 818; NP 1046
[OOR 1816, Rd 1924f & 2011f; Pr 640]

28. Thu. Thursday of the 34th Week in Ordinary Time
MP 824; DP 1012; EP 830; NP 1049
[OOR 1819, Rd 1924f & 2011f; Pr 640]

29. Fri. Friday of the 34th Week in Ordinary Time
MP 835; DP 1017; EP 840; NP 1052
[OOR 1821, Rd 1924f & 2011f; Pr 640]

30. Sat. ST. ANDREW, AP (F) 1325
MP 1325 (707); DP 1022; EP (41) 701; NP 1034
[OOR 1824, Rd 1924f & 2043f; TD Pr 1327]

DECEMBER

1. **Sun. FIRST SUNDAY OF ADVENT 43**
MP (43) 707; DP 994; EP (45) 712; NP 1037
[OOR 1785, Rd 1870f & 1942f; TD Pr 44]

2. Mon. Monday of the 1st Week of Advent
MP (47) 718; DP 998; EP (48) 723; NP 1041
[OOR 1788, Rd 1870f & 1942f; Pr 48]

3. Tue. St. Francis Xavier, P (Mem) 1329
MP (1426) 728; DP 1003; EP (1430) 734; NP 1044
[OOR 1791, Rd 1870f & 2046f; Pr 1329]

4. Wed. Advent Weekday or St. John Damascene, P & D (1330)
   MP (1435) (53) 738; DP 1008; EP (1436) (54) 743; NP 1046
   [OOR 1794, Rd 1870f & 2046f; Pr 1330 or 54]

5. Thu. Thursday of the 1st Week of Advent
   MP (56) 748; DP 1012; EP (57) 754; NP 1049
   [OOR 1797, Rd 1870f & 1942f; Pr 57]

6. Fri. Advent Weekday or St. Nicholas, B (1330)
   MP (1426) (59) 759; DP 1017; EP (1430) (60) 765; NP 1052
   [OOR 1800, Rd 1870f & 1942f or 2046f; Pr 1331 or 60]

7. Sat. St. Ambrose, B & D (Mem) 1331
   MP (1435) 770; DP 1022; EP (64) 775; NP 1034
   [OOR 1802, Rd 1870f & 2046f; Pr 1331]

8. **Sun. SECOND SUNDAY OF ADVENT 66**
   MP (66) 780; DP 994; EP (68) 786; NP 1037
   [OOR 1806, Rd 1870f & 1942f; TD Pr 67]

9. Mon. IMMACULATE CONCEPTION (Sol) 1334 (not a Holyday of Obligation)
   MP 1334 (707); DP 1027; EP 1336 (1378); NP 1037
   [OOR 1809, Rd 1870f & 1951f; TD Pr 1336]

10. Tue. Advent Weekday or Our Lady of Loreto *(New)* (1372)
    MP (1372) (73) 802; DP 1003; EP (1378) (74) 807; NP 1044
    [OOR 1812, Rd 1870f & 1942f or 1951f; Pr 74 or 38 in this Guide]

11. Wed. Advent Weekday or St. Damasus I, Po (1339)
    MP (1426) (76) 812; DP 1008; EP (1430) (77) 818; NP 1046
    [OOR 1816, Rd 1870f & 1942f or 2046f; Pr 1339 or 77]

12. Thu. OUR LADY OF GUADALUPE (F) **(New)** (33) or 1339
    MP (42) & 1372 (707); DP 1012; EP (46) & 1378, Pr (48); NP 1049
    [OOR (34) & 1819, Rd 1870f & 1951f; TD Pr (42) or 1340]

13. Fri. St. Lucy, V & M (Mem) 1341
    MP (1414 or 1441) (Ant) 835; DP 1017
    EP (1417 or 1444) (Ant) 840; NP 1052
    [OOR 1821, Rd 1870f & 2045f; Pr 1341]

14. Sat. St. John of the Cross, P & D (Mem) 1342
    MP (1435) 845; DP 1022; EP (87) 851; NP 1034
    [OOR 1824, Rd 1870f & 2046f; Pr 1342]

15. **Sun. THIRD SUNDAY OF ADVENT 89**
    MP (89) 856; DP 994; EP (91) 861; NP 1037
    [OOR 1827, Rd 1870f & 1942f; TD Pr 91]

16. Mon. Monday of the 3rd Week of Advent
    MP (94) 867; DP 998; EP (95) 872; NP 1041
    [OOR 1829, Rd 1870f & 1942f; Pr 95]

17. Tue. Tuesday of the 3rd Week of Advent
    MP (116) 877; DP 1003; EP (117) 882; NP 1044
    [OOR 1831, Rd 1870f & 1942f; Pr 117]

18. Wed. Wednesday of the 3rd Week of Advent
    MP (119) 886; DP 1008; EP (120) 892; NP 1046
    [OOR 1835, Rd 1870f & 1942f; Pr 120]

19. Thu. Thursday of the 3rd Week of Advent
    MP (122) 897; DP 1012; EP (123) 901; NP 1049
    [OOR 1838, Rd 1870f & 1942f, Pr 123]

20. Fri. Friday of the 3rd Week of Advent
    MP (125) 906; DP 1017; EP (126) 911; NP 1052
    [OOR 1842, Rd 1870f & 1942f; Pr 126]

21. Sat. Saturday of the 3rd Week of Advent
    MP (128) 916 (St. Peter Canisius, P & D 1343); DP 1022
    EP (110) 921; NP 1034
    [OOR 1845, Rd 1870f & 1942f; Pr 1343 or 129]

22. **Sun. FOURTH SUNDAY OF ADVENT 111**
    MP (112) 925 (Ant 132); DP 994; EP (114) 931 (Ant 133); NP 1037
    [OOR 1850, Rd 1870f & 1942f; TD Pr 113]

23. Mon. Monday of the 4th Week of Advent
    MP (134) 937 (St. John of Kanty, P 1344); DP 998
    EP (136) 942 (St. John of Kanty, P 1344); NP 1041
    [OOR 1853, Rd 1870f & 1942f; Pr 1344 or 135]

24. Tue. Tuesday of the 4th Week of Advent
    MP (137) 947; DP 1003; EP 140; NP 1034
    [OOR 1856, Rd 1870f & 1942f; Pr 139]

25. **Wed. CHRISTMAS (Sol) 144**
    MP 144 (707); DP 1027; EP 147; NP 1034 or 1037
    [OOR 1859, Rd 1882f & 1955f; TD Pr 146]

26. Thu. ST. STEPHEN, FIRST MARTYR (F) 1344
MP 1345 (707); DP 1012; EP 147 & 159; NP 1034 or 1037
[OOR 1861, Rd 1882f & 1957f; TD Pr 1346]

27. Fri. ST. JOHN, AP & EVANGELIST (F) 1347
MP 1347 (707); DP 1017; EP 147 & 161; NP 1034 or 1037
[OOR 1864, Rd 1882f & 1959f; TD Pr 1348]

28. Sat. HOLY INNOCENTS, MM (F) 1349
MP 1349 (707); DP 1022; EP 152 (1368); NP 1034 or 1037
[OOR 1867, Rd 1882f & 1961f; TD Pr 1351]

29. **Sun. HOLY FAMILY (F) 154**
MP 154 (707); DP 994; EP 156 (1378); NP 1034 or 1037
[OOR 1785, Rd 1882f & 1955f; TD Pr 156]

30. Mon. SIXTH DAY IN THE OCTAVE OF CHRISTMAS
MP 144 & 168; DP 998; EP 147 & 169; NP 1034 or 1037
[OOR 1788, Rd 1882f & 1955f; TD Pr 169]

31. Tue. SEVENTH DAY IN THE OCTAVE OF CHRISTMAS
MP 144 & 171 (St. Sylvester I, Po 1353); DP 1003
EP 173 (1368); NP 1034 or 1037
[OOR 1791, Rd 1882f & 1955f; TD Pr 1353 or 172]

Prayers

(For use on December 10, Our Lady of Loreto
[Optional Memorial])

O God, who, fulfilling the promise made to our Fathers,
chose the Blessed Virgin Mary
to become the Mother of the Savior,
grant that we may follow her example,
for her humility was pleasing to you
and her obedience profitable to us.
Through our Lord Jesus Christ, your Son,
who lives and reigns with you in the unity of the Holy Spirit,
God, for ever and ever.

709/13

LITURGY OF THE HOURS

This is the official English edition of the Divine Office that contains the translation approved by the International Commission on English in the Liturgy.

No. 409/10 Set of 4 volumes
ISBN 978-0-89942-409-5

No. 409/13 Set of 4 volumes—Black Leather Binding
Note: available in sets only
ISBN 978-0-89942-411-8

No. 709/13 Set of 4 volumes—Large Print, Leather Binding. *Note: available in sets only*
ISBN 978-0-89942-710-2

409/10

409/13

41

A Companion to the Liturgy of the Hours:
Morning and Evening Prayer

By Shirley Darcus Sullivan

A spiritual companion for Morning and Evening Prayer of the Four-Week Psalter. It presents ways in which the experience of the Hours may be made more prayerful for those who say them, e.g., by using the spirituality of Carmel, especially that of Elizabeth of the Trinity. 208 pages. Size 5½ x 8¼. Flexible full-color paper cover.

No. 415/04
ISBN: 978-0-89942-432-3

The Divine Office for Dodos

A Step-by-Step Guide to Praying the Liturgy of the Hours

By Madeline Pecora Nugent

For those who want to pray all the Hours correctly and completely, this book contains over 90 detailed lessons with questions, helpful hints, and practice sessions presented in a simple style. 272 pages. Size $5^{1}/_{4}$ x $7^{3}/_{4}$.

No. 416/04
ISBN: 978-0-89942-482-8

"There is hope in these pages! You are going to learn to pray the Divine Office! Honest! Then you will join the ranks of other clergy, religious, and laity, some of whom are non-Catholic, who pray the Divine Office every day."

—From the Author's Introduction

PRACTICAL GUIDE FOR THE LITURGY OF THE HOURS

PRACTICAL GUIDE FOR THE LITURGY OF THE HOURS—By Shirley Sullivan. This book begins with a treatment of the two main Hours of Morning and Evening Prayer and then also presents the other Hours. It offers guidance to individuals as well as for groups to pray in a rich and meaningful way. 96 pages. Size $4^3/_8$ x $6^3/_4$.

No. 426/04—Flexible cover ISBN 978-0-89942-484-2

COMPANION PRAYER BOOK TO THE LITURGY OF THE HOURS

COMPANION PRAYER BOOK TO THE LITURGY OF THE HOURS—By Georges-Albert Boissinot. This book is meant to help all clergy, religious, and lay people to share more fully in the Prayer of the Church through inspirational prayers and reflections centered on the celebration of the Hours. 128 pages. Size $4^3/_8$ x $6^3/_4$.

No. 434/04—Flexible cover ISBN 978-0-89942-354-8

OTHER OUTSTANDING CATHOLIC BOOKS

HOLY BIBLE—The Saint Joseph Edition of the **NEW CATHOLIC BIBLE (NCB)** is a fresh, faithful, and reader-friendly translation. All editions are intended to be used by Catholics for daily prayer and meditation, as well as private devotion and group study. The editions feature Large, Readable Type, Rich Explanatory Notes, Maps, Photographs, a section entitled "Learning about Your Bible," and a Doctrinal Bible Index.

Family Edition	**No. 619**
Giant Type Edition	**No. 617**

NEW TESTAMENT—St. Joseph Edition of the **NEW CATHOLIC BIBLE** translation. Large, easy-to-read type, with helpful Notes and Maps. Features the words of Christ in red.

Vest Pocket Edition	**No. 650**
Study Edition—Includes many helps.	**No. 311**
Pocket Edition—Illustrated. (Christ's words not in red.)	**No. 630**

THE PSALMS—St. Joseph **NEW CATHOLIC BIBLE,** printed in large, easy-to-read type with copious informative notes and cross-references.

	No. 665

OTHER OUTSTANDING CATHOLIC BOOKS

St. Joseph SUNDAY MISSAL—Complete Edition . . . in accord with *The Roman Misssal*, Third Edition. Includes all 3 Cycles (**A, B, and C**) with explanations. 1,600 pages. **No. 820**

St. Joseph WEEKDAY MISSAL (Vol. I & II)—All the Mass texts needed for weekdays in accord with *The Roman Misssal*, Third Edition. An indispensable aid for all who celebrate and participate at daily Mass.
Nos. 920 & 921
Large Type Edition **Nos. 922 & 923**

St. Joseph SUNDAY MISSAL—LARGE TYPE EDITION—Includes the Readings for the 3-year Cycle printed in extra-large type for easy reading. Includes full-color inserts. **No. 822**

St. Joseph CHURCH HISTORY—Sets forth the major events in the life of the Church in a clear and logical fashion that makes them understandable to the modern reader. Large type. Illustrated. **No. 262**

BIBLE MEDITATIONS FOR EVERY DAY—By Rev. John C. Kersten, S.V.D. Excellent aid for daily meditation. A Scripture passage and a short, invaluable introduction are given for every day. **No. 277**

MARY DAY BY DAY—Introduction by Rev. Charles G. Fehrenbach, C.SS.R. Minute Marian meditations for every day of the year, including a Scripture passage, a quotation from the Saints, and a concluding prayer. Over 300 illustrations in two colors. **No. 180**

NEW SAINT JOSEPH PEOPLE'S PRAYER BOOK—Edited by Rev. Francis Evans. An encyclopedia of prayers, drawn from the Bible and Liturgy, the *Enchiridion of Indulgences*, the Saints and spiritual writers—plus hundreds of traditional and contemporary prayers for every need. Over 1,400 prayers typeset in sense lines. Large type. Printed and illustrated in two colors. 1,056 pages. **No. 900**

FOLLOWING THE HOLY SPIRIT—By Rev. Walter van de Putte, C.S.Sp. Patterned after *The Imitation of Christ*, it contains dialogues with, and prayers to, the Holy Spirit. Large type. Illustrated. **No. 335**

MARY MY HOPE—By Rev. Lawrence G. Lovasik, S.V.D. Popular book of devotions to Mary. Large type. Illustrated. **No. 365**

The
LITURGY OF THE HOURS
is truly the prayer of the Church
for all the people of God —
bishops, priests, deacons,
religious and the
laity.

ISBN 978-1-958237-14-4

This Guide is No. 406/G
ISBN 978-1-958237-14-4